Epistles from the Drifters 1

World Poems

Yongjea John Han

Copyright © 2018 Yongjea John Han

First edition

Designed and Edited by World Letters Press Poetry

All rights reserved. No part of this book may be reproduced or transmitted in any form or by any means, electronic or mechanical, including photocopying, recording, or by any information storage or retrieval system, without the prior written permission of World Letters Press.

ISBN-13: 978-1-7750387-5-7

CONTENTS

PART 1

The United Arab Emirates 8
Armenia 10
Azerbaijan 13
Abkhazia 15
Yemen 17
Oman 19
Jordan 21
Iraq 23
Israel 25
Georgia 28
Qatar 31
Kuwait 33
Cyprus 35
Turkey 38
South Ossetia 40
Lebanon 42
Bahrain 44
Northern Cyprus 47
Saudi Arabia 50
Syria 53
Palestine 56
Korea 58
Japan 60
China 64
India 70
Mongolia 75
Philippines 78
Indonesia 81

Sri Lanka **81**

PART 2

Myanmar **86**
Vietnam **88**
Cambodia **91**
Laos **93**
Tibet **95**
Bhutan **97**
Nepal **99**
Bangladesh **101**
Malaysia **103**
Taiwan **105**
Singapore **107**
Hong Kong **109**
Thailand **110**
Pakistan **113**
Kazakhstan **114**
Afghanistan **116**
Uzbekistan **118**
Kyrgyzstan **120**
Tajikistan **122**
Turkmenistan **124**
Brunei **127**
Timor-Leste, East Timor **129**
Maldive Islands **131**
Iran **133**
Artsakh Republic **136**

# PART 1

The United Arab Emirates

I will remember the day
when the door opens there,
all the boundaries are broken,
and the word is rooted.
When we see the saints
we meet in the desert,
we remember the time
when we let the water of life spring
from the cracks of the rocks
and drink the water of life.
If we follow the footsteps of the steps
that bring good news,
we'll be in a happy country.
We will meet with a man
who will ride on a donkey
that is not tired and come on his way.
Do not forget the day
that the little valley is filled
and the blue stream rises again.
We will be friends there on the day
when the door is wide open.

2

We will meet the dawn on the road
without any obstacles on the right way.

There, where there will be no fear,
on the truth that will not fall,
we will set the cross,
we will sing to the scattered people.
The darkness can not win the light.
We will gather in the square,
sing the triumph of victory,
face the faces of our loved ones
and friends in front of the fallen fence
and open door.

3

The visible world is not everything.
There will be a kingdom that will never be seen,
and he who has the evidence of victory
in both hands
and feet will always be awaiting us from there,

Armenia

As I climbed the mountain
and looked everywhere,
the traces and teachings of the apostles
sounded like echoes.
We can not forget the old city.
In a square where beautiful love songs ring,
freedom, joy and liberation shout,
young lovers sing love.
I will remember the saints who went eastward
beyond the high mountain
when the wind blowing
in the fields of the reeds
and the blessed news of the clear waters flowing
in the brook in front of the village.
Armenia, let's not forget the day of blooming
like the flowers of martyr for the world that is
always there.

2

Do not forget the pilgrims
who remember the good people
of your country and mountain villages,
like a salmon looking for
a hometown after a long journey.
As the birds of the golden field

are filled with riches,
the nests of every little tree are made,
and the birds preparing the blessed shelter,
there will be no one to rise above this country,
and the humble ones will enter the land.
What a splendid land!
The Holy Land of Faith!

3

Blessed is the grace of the Lord
to come again to the land,
and will gladden us;
I look upon the most honorable day
as a loyal steward.
The traces of the tears will not be disappeared
to the rugged mountain valley.
The lament that calls at the mountain
become your strong voice
and those who sleep in the land will wake up
and prepare a new day.

4

On the day that the fallen lands are restored,
the days when all the enemies retreat,
the day the peace comes to the land,
the songs of the children ringing everywhere,
the youthful generation and the future

where the dream will not disappear,
And always remember the splendor of spring,
passion like summer,
sublime elegance like autumn,
and tranquility like winter, Armenian!

Azerbaijan

Do not forget the days
when you wanted to cleanse your mind
and deepen your memories of a glorious culture
that has awakened from its long nightmares
and return to that experience.
What was the cry for?
We want to be a boy who
will not be afraid of change
until we reaching the top of a hill
as high as the independence
and freedom of the people,
and the shout of victory is delivered
to the end of the continent.
The day of hope will come when to set the cross
and to pray in the temple of repentance.
The small chalice floating
in the east will never sink
in front of any storm.
Our beloved home!

2

I see brave riders.
Look at the dignified position.
With the courageous stiffness
and will of the uninhibited,

the land of the horseshoe sounded
for thousands of years.
When we wake up those who sleep
by the cry of the wise man
and the strong spirit of the past,
we will set the cornerstone
and meet the era of reconstruction.

3

We will soon meet those who have come running
without a long way on their independence.
We hope they are blessed words.
The blessed word of salvation
from the fate of all to die
will soon come out of here like living water.
Those who survived the day with a strong will!
Let us wait together and be saved from despair.

Abkhazia

There is no resting place in the land
where sad souls are buried; Where did you go?
Nostalgic villagers!
To find the soul's innocence,
they came back to their hometown,
and there was no sound.
They could not remember
the faces of the children
they saw in their childhood.
Do not forget your warmest cup of tea
for your best friend.
We're looking for the back of a boy
who has just passed away for independence.
Abkhazia,
we want you to be a country of tolerance,
a tune of souls so that you can make your way on rough mountains
so that one can climb this road together.

2

Can you feel a little vibration? Abkhazia, people.
Where the source of the tremors came from,
the combinations of eager desires
were never far from us.
Listen to them, the whispers of souls,

and the movement of their little wishes
to live with each other.
At that time we will find that the deepest sea,
the mountain and
the river flowing quietly can be ours.
We'll wait for that.
In this place, each other will become a shield
and live with dependence.

3

We will remember the names
and activities of this place
and will tell people who will live here
in the distant future.
We tried to keep the soul that did not fall down
and the attachment of the living in the spirit.
We will call the name of the stranger
who will come to life on this earth for a while
and we will be ready for that day now
that I am sure that we are still alive.

Yemen

How many stories had to be done over the years?
They set the night together and counted the stars
and comforted those
who were tired of long journeys
on the way to the continent in many stories.
Look at the rich river flowing west.
When you give sorghum, cotton, and mango
from the river of the living water
and give it to the brethren,
you will always receive soul harvest.

2

We are going to meet old friends there,
so we will not be afraid of the rough mountains
and the desert.
We will recall the days of dreaming
to harvest the abundant grain
from the barren land.
Children in rural villages will recover laughing
and strong young men will fix the wall fallen
down and the road.
We will plant an olive tree on the roadside
and smell a fragrant smile.
Ah! Who will meet him in the clouds?
The time will come again

to keep the innocence of the crowd
to welcome them.

3

Would you listen to those stories again?
I want the mind to be humble and low
and always ready to hear.
Keep in mind that we can move forward
as much as we prepare
and the fact that it is done as we think.
Open your eyes, ears, and mouth,
and the stories that passed by then will not
return to the fruit that is not in vain,
in the future land.

Oman

Let's go to the broad gardens with its flap
on the eastern end and the woolly silk.
The wreckage of the red stone
that's scattered all over the place
tells us a story that's still too small.
Where is that boundary?
People who crossed the border
and went to the eastern country.
They resemble the eyes of a pure white camel,
counting the years they have been together
and singing songs that everyone knows.
We climbed up the mountain,
to which the desert struck,
and we knew that our boundary
was not there either.
Where are the poor?
Stand on that red plain.

2

Listen to the sound heard in the wind.
We know there will be a festival of reconciliation
and forgiveness not far from here.
We know that our summer will be waiting for
the abundant mineral water
and the plentiful winter.

We will no longer have riders with grief,
but with astute eyes wait for our deliverer
in the bushes of the desert.
Let's put away perversity
from the eyes and mouth.
Our voice shall be the prayer of the righteous,
and we must guard this stronghold.

3

Let the idols of man be forsaken,
and forget it.
It's just like the scenery that passes by the
seasons is different.
It's like a sand dune disappears for a while.
Everything changes easily.
Like doing nothing at the deep night,
no one can carry on.
I have to wait until the bright morning comes.
Do not let small things stay in vain.
The heritage we have to harvest is only
discarding idols
and denying vain beliefs,

Jordan

Madaba,
headed for an ancient city painted on murals.
When their passion for a new land is gathered
and they cross over the mountain
without barricades,
we find a fresh spring water for every people
and we hope for the land we dreamed of.
The shelter will be there for those who have
unbuttoned the border
and missed their freedom.
We will meet people who are not lonely in
untiring pace, art, and passion.

2

Where will you go along the firm rock?
When we read the old characters
waiting in the dead end,
we take back the mistakes and see the future.
You will see a procession of long and distant
people in the desert terrain
where the water does not dry.
The cold of the night will always prepare to come,
so any little life that lives here will find
its way forward.
I hope you will be the home of

those who have a thirst
and those who have lost their homes.

3

Do not turn away from
those who come to the strange land
beyond the border.
We are all witnesses.
Crossing the border is another harvest for
abandonment and frustration.
Let's not forget the glorious days of civilization.
It is a nation surrounded by gorgeous
embellishments and gold cloths,
and it is necessary to remember
the blessed people
who have crossed mountains
and rivers on horseback.
No matter where it is,
every land that you step on will have clear marks
and traces, and a day will come when you will
hold your brother
and sister on the same day.

Iraq

Have you gone to sleep,
Tigris and the Euphrates?
As the sunny rain poured out of the sky,
On the serene surface of the water many
thousands of years of grief
and compassion danced
like characters written in the papers
that were replying.
The children who grew up
looking at the cracked land wandered
because they could not find a place to go
because of losing their country
in the frozen tundra.
To forget their trace is to silence
another injustice.

2

Now we have to finish all this conflict.
You should know that there is a time
when the long winter time
that has come down to the mountain passes.
When we sort out what we have to throw away,
the day will come when we will be able to look
back at the pain of
those who have fallen.

The age of chaos and division must go.
You can escape poverty.
One day this long journey will end soon.

3

Look around for the lost one.
People who come back from all places
and live in the house that restored!
Still, brethren, bear their terrible times
and cross the sea,
and see that the last line of life will not be cut off.
Winter will not be so cold.
When all the lost will return home,
the spring will come,
and the river of Eden will soon be overflowing
again.

Israel

David's star,
who has finished a long silent training,
is still praying for the union of the divided land,
where the direction of the light is now,
and seeing those who stand before the wall.
The lamb went to the distant wilderness road,
but when will this still unhealed place be comforted?
You should not forget that day.
The day when the stars of the sky
will pour like a meteor,
the grave will be opened and the hymn of
triumph will be echoed.

2

When they were lost
in the midst of the wilderness,
they met an oasis of flow of life
with the guidance of a kind man.
They said. We will not go in the wrong way again.
The desert will reap olive
and plentiful grapefruit,
and the lake of Galilee will offer fat fish
and peaceful silence, a traveler who will go a
long way!

Let's lay down your load and walk along the
flower path.
Let's have a dream of a young man
when peace comes to an end
after a dispute and quarreling.

3

We will see the abundant fruit in the vineyard.
Break the fence into the plantation
and make a beautiful garden
for everyone to go in.
No one is lost in it.
The weaker ones are even better.
Who are the chosen people?
They are the ones who come back
from a long way
in front of a wooden crucifix
and rest their weary bodies.
There will be no discrimination and indifference.
Those who rely on one another
and who can send living water
to those who have fallen,
are the chosen ones.
There you will know that all are brothers.

4

How would you forget such a lost person?

One must bury the abandoned chagrin
and sorrow in the deep ground.
People will wait.
The people who are closest to us
and those who have hurt each other
by joining enemies await us.
We remember the blessed Sabbath day
to be healed.
Was this close to each other?
We will always be chosen in a garden
with plenty of fruit,
and a day of enjoying the boundaries will soon
come through you.

Georgia

On a day when a red rose is rising, in our eyes,
we will return to a more mature adult age
and see the spires boasting of on the hill.
My old friend, where have you been
and what have you been doing?
Your face resembled the robustness
and the vitality courage.
Like honey bees flying
in beautiful flower fields to find honey!
O!, on that day all sorrow and labor will end.
Georgia! My brother!
Do not forget the shout that shouted together!
Always, justice is our side,

2

Our hearts are still in the wide field.
Do not forget that there is a space for all of us
who fill us up every year
so that our food is not lacking.
On the day when all of us will gather together
and have a pleasant dining table,
we will be accompanied
by the fullness of the soul
and the satisfaction of life so that this trip will
not be lonely until that day.

Georgia!
A port to cross a river of oppression to a secure place

3

The comrades who have been there will be waiting for us,
and never fear the voyage.
Through the heart of the boy,
we will walk across the sea
and follow the mountains with our love
and commitment to an intense life.
Georgia!
We want to keep our last faith.
Always remember that belief is the representation of our soul,
the witnesses who tried to capture it.
The wind cannot beat the stars, the moon,
and the sun. As we are always there,
we can go this way if we do not tremble.

4

We wait for the day when the tears on our cheeks will be stopped.
We hold a garland of joy in both hands
we stand on the hill that everyone knows.
And listen to the rhythm of the emancipation

that is heard in the wind.
We who wait for the near of us
who comfort the weak,
We can pass through the deep
and wide rivers without fear,
And the snow-capped mountain peaks
will fly like eagles.
When we wake up, we will all be one.
The day to call our name was not far.

Qatar

Qatar Doha The final destination of the sun,
the bridge of desire for Europe We stand there.
I have seen people who have been waiting for
tens of thousands of years
and are looking for the lost truth.
I saw the movements that rose again
in front of the passion.
In the last resistance that never shaken,
the flower in the desert is about to bloom.
I see the pearl of the sea.
It was the will of people who shone
like a jewel in one spot.

2

Do not be afraid to stand in the center.
When the border collapses,
discrimination will leave
and let's hold the joyful toast together.
The river of life will flow in the dry desert.
We will always enjoy the abundance
of the fruit of the good tree.
Everyone once gets a rest in the garden of the air,
and there they sow a seed to enrich the soul.

3

**We hope that the freshness of the pearl of the sea
and its bright colors do not change all the time,
but also as we approach those
who look for it in various ways.
We hope that dreams and fantasies
you had are not lies.
We crossed Doha that way.
Leaving a little leisurely space
in the dry ground like a little rain.**

Kuwait

The Persian Gulf,
I'm going to find the way to the oasis,
the unknown land with nine jewels on the ocean.
Teach me the way to the fertile ground here.
We are now lost in the vast,
flat and desolate desert.
In the Persian Gulf,
in the tens of thousands of years,
with the untouched beauty of the hidden coast,
we will find a way to get there sometime in a
shallow wave.

2

The long, cold night has passed.
Now the warm sun comes up in the east
and the hours of hibernation
we built last night will wake up.
Then friends! We should not be scattered,
but to gather together to see the sun over the gulf.
Sing the names of the families
who have gone away.
Crossing the sea,
we will return to you with presents
full of two arms,
that day was not far.

It was a long night, was not it?
Because there is hope for tomorrow,
we know the importance of life today.
Do not forget Kuwait,
which is always quiet
and looking at new days.

3

When the equatorial nations want
to be at the center of it,
even the earth's ends will be blessed.
The mind has always been there.
When the passersby stop
and ask for directions to it,
one will lose the wall of prejudice
and teach the way to open up the heart.
When we cross the desert
and pass through the gravel,
and see the plain that has been turned
into an oak,
we will stand on our feet and stand on the way,
and we will meet the guests from all the way.
We can not forget that night.
We wonder if there was such a mild night,
maybe a long journey to find a way to go there.

Cyprus

Troodos, the hometown of the gods,
blew the flute on the hill.
Was it a beautiful melody night?
The shaking of the serene bushes
and the freshness of
the early morning came unceasingly.
We want you to be comforted now
with the firmness of broken land
and river and scattered brethren.
We always miss the land of hometown.
We cannot forget the fragrance of the olive tree
that we climbed with our house yard.
Cyprus, we want to sing in a dense forest.
We wanted to be a comfort for visitors
who do not know any name.

2

One day we know that the stars in the sky
do not always disappear but keep their place.
As it is, we will be sure
that someday we will become one body
and keep our family together.
Brothers! and Aunts!
who came back from the front wielding
with the red skirt!

Nobody knows when it will be,
but we have to keep this land
with a firm conviction.
Look at the eyes of our growing children.
The clear lake should flow
through the rough road
where there is a flow of soothing
and hearty beatings.
The beautiful land of Cyprus,
we will wait for the day
when the land will wake up
from the deep sleep.

3

I stand on a hill
where all the little towns are visible.
On a day when the warm
southerly wind is blowing,
on the day when all the fresh flowers
come on the wind.
Now I know how blessed
it is not to lose hope in this place.
Passionate people!
With the pure enthusiasm,
the day will come for being one again,
and I will climb a small hill, dancing with joy
and singing victory.
That day will come soon.

**Day when all boundaries collapse,
day when discrimination and despair disappear**

Turkey

In the old library,
it seemed as if there was still a terrible
and tumultuous shout.
The lands crumbled and hid in deep caves,
enduring all kinds of persecutions
and years of indignation.
The brothers who were so fatigued were
never scared.
In the back of the tragic history of strong
but nobody was afraid,
I saw the back of a young man waiting
for the final judgment.
I stood with the impossibility
and the unflinching truth.
Now I have to listen to their voices.
They should not have forsaken the true things.
But all that's left is the lonely crescent moon in
the night sky.

2

Throw away the wild blade
and you must cross the oceans
with softness and gentleness.
The cold and the wind
that seems to be lifting will soon come to an end,

and the strength to stand up with
the sword will not always meet
and will run parallel,
will we ever face them?
I look at the stones that are still dull in Ephesus
for thousands of years.
Listen to their whispers buried
in the limestone cave of Cappadocia.
I hear the martyrs of the catacombs.
The days that were gorgeous and missed remain
a trail.

3

Looks like the wheels of a dug on a marble road
as if to run into the history of thousands of years.
I followed the trail to people all over the place
and buried the collection of civilization here.
We remember. I want you to know here
that there is no longer any old leather bag to
hold a new one.
You can see humility by looking down
at the lower back for once.
Someday it will be shared
and everyone will be happy.
Like a yellow flower blooming in a field,
a bright spring will come to a wide plain.

South Ossetia

In the winter, we should remember
those who have crossed the Caucasus Mountains
and missed their freedom,
and who have left for warm southerly winds.
When will it come to the time
when it gathered together
at the table with the face which was always sweet
and was laughing and sharing
with the warm food
which mother made?
The young men who flooded
the streets could not return
beyond the snow-covered mountain range.
Do not forget the days
when you were poor but your mind was rich.
This is not a wilderness without water.
You are always alive
because of the flow of good life in deep heart!
Do not forget. That you are always
walking this way together,
that your mother and family
are still waiting in front of the door,

2

Still, the water flowing
from the top of the mountain
was not always dry, and it was still reaching
where our brothers live.
They lived in a garden that was so beautiful
as the trees of the green season were rooted
on the rivers and like flowers in the fields.
Like a clear deep fountain in the mountains,
Ossetia, your name will be
the breath of the Asian continent
so that they can rest a night as if they were tired
of a long trip,

Lebanon

The emerald shoreline that stretches straight up,
in the light of that thinness,
you can see that grandeur that has kept it there
for thousands of years.
Look at the whole body of dabke dancing
enthusiastically to music.
The beautiful figure resembled a solid cedar
that stretched out thick and straight into the sky.
It was a mighty force that did not yield to any
subtle spirit.
Becharreh, Arz Ar-rab, meeting the people
who raise the pillars of the temple
and raise prayers
in the majestic Kadisha Gorge,
letting them know
that there are some unshakeable spirits here.
Brothers of Lebanon,
Let' s go to that lush cedar forest.
Hold the pearls of the Middle East in your arms,
and build the temple of God under
every pouring starlight.
In the presence of silent silence,
those who visit will be friends.

2

If you go to the magnificent forests,
there are a lot of friends who wanted to meet
in the stories that were heard
among the trees for thousands of years.
Those who have roots to
the bottom of the deep lake
and have always been able to breathe
with the clear water of life, Lebanon,
tomorrow will probably be such a day.
The desert is not a borderline world that could
not be crossed.

3

We met saints in Lebanon who built a temple
and built a house in a beautiful place.
Wearing white as light as fleece,
they crossed the desert and showed the way to
those who came here.
They always say: Look at those trees.
It is said that we will do our lives as well as
the straightened minds without the curves
and that the small flowers blooming
in the fields sing
according to those days. Lebanon,
to be a resting place and a cry for
those who are always weary at the border.

Bahrain

We must be prepared to accept
a pure white bride who has crossed the two seas.
The innocent should reach and set a new tent
above the barren wilderness, waiting for the day
when they can sing freely
and be free from all past traditions of the past.
Boy! Do not spend your most passionate days
in vain like the depths of morning and night.
Imagine the appearance of a bride wearing
uncomplicated clothes and waiting for the
bridegroom.
Let's wake up from an old sleep
and meet a new morning of the Persian Gulf.
We will surely meet you then,
just as we can not predict the appearance of a
sand dune overnight.

2

I could not pass any of them.
The news of those who crossed
the sea of ungodliness
and landed on the shore was buried
in the grave of an ancient king,
but people saw hope in an empty net
that was constantly rolling up.

If this was not a jail without a grate,
I hope you open the door of your firmly closed mind.
Friend! Where are we going now?
When are we going to lift up the minds of the imagination
that will not perish like the fragments
of small pieces of plastic floating in the sea?

3

What line should I take?
There is always peace in the deep sea.
Let the pieces of small droplets gather together
to give water to the garden of life,
and to have a room to eat a rich meal of one.
My beloved brothers are gathering together
and laughing at each other, singing and dancing.
When the warm breeze blows in the Gulf,
memories of a young day bloom like a flower!
As we walk through every corner of a small island,
buried our passion and effort,
fly like a bird lightly walk
wherever you are.
We still wait here for him.
The time is not boring
My beautiful days are always here
to walk in the sea with a crush like a virgin!

4

Like an herb flower beneath
a house garden fence,
it bloomed under the hot sunlight
of the Middle East.
It is now time to go together.
It was time to send out strangers
who were trapped in all the halls.
The traces of those who have gone
through this land will not be erased.
When unfamiliar things become familiar,
their innocent faces and humor still hovering
in their ears have become memories that we
must reap.

Northern Cyprus

We stand facing the walls.
The night in Kyrenia was so deep and long.
The people who were sleeping together
and we talked all night talking about
the song and the shouting of those who
were trapped in the walls,
and who was desperately seeking
independence from whom.
We had to go to the Sophia Cathedral
for repentance for the past and kneel to hear
the comforts of the many who came here.
When can you meet the people who are
breathing here
and discussing in the square?
We go to the harbor every night
and look at the distant sea covered in darkness.
In the depths of our minds and in the world of
thought
we know who is waiting for us.
Northern Cyprus!
Do not forget.
Our freedom is still waiting there,

2

Little prophet!

**Blow up the flute on a wide hill
overlooking the sea!
Life is not heavy for
those who come across that sea,
and it will always be a pleasure to greet guests
from all sides with a splendid season.
The day will come when your name
will be called to everyone.
If we lightly walked this road together,
we would all gather together
in this square to gather together
singing, dancing, sharing food, liberating,
Nostalgic faces!**

3

**In the morning of the resurrection
from the crowd,
Troodos Massif where the first sound heard,
where the clouds
and the wind stopped for a while,
we stand there.
Do not look back!
Good sailors!
When your ships are tied to a distant harbor
and you climb along the line,
our square will be waiting for you.
Let's not forget the shout.**

Looking at the sound of the shepherd's whistle
turning round
and around my ear
and my consciousness to wake up,
We found that all the moments
were the happiest time,

Saudi Arabia

We got lost in Rub'al Khali.
The desert houses that
we built together last night
in a lighter sand wind than
our thoughts are lost together.
What pilgrims should we wait for
in the empty space?
Looking at the stars that
have poured down a long time ago,
I saw the ruins of this white blank land
and looked at the temple
and talked about
the many kingdoms of long time ago.
Our shadows standing here
together are all friends.
The country of imagination and speculation,
I will never forget that face. On the rainy day,
let us build the house of imagination again.
Let's dig a well in the garden of the house
and make a garden where roses bloom.
On that day when anyone can remember.

2

Do not forget what is in your hands.
Do not forget to walk through this long,

long deserted pathway to the oasis of deep water
without red blood.
Nobody will be discriminated against in the land.
The best being is to inform our living
and future children that we are here.
Everyone on the day of equality
will be able to realize
that the dreams we had were not empty-handed
when the closed doors open
and many people come back here again.
We will get the way we wanted so much here,
on that day,

3

I will be waiting here for the warm
and mild spring day of freedom.
When all veils are cut off
and there is a wall-free fellowship
with the people,
the sheep that are kept in us wait for the day
to go their own way in search of green pastures.
We will have a small shelter
where we can stay where we are
when we are deeply moved
in the heart of the day
when the road in the desert will be preserved.
I will not forget your beautiful appearance.
Tonight I will not sleep on the cold floor,

feeling the fresh sunlight of the morning,
let's share the story freely
over the night holding one flower
you do not know the name on this roadside.
Until the desert saint comes to visit us soon.

Syria

Here we are trying to recover
the grand and old territory.
Damascus, recalling the encounter
and excitement of the scene,
we read a blurred wall letters written
in the hands of a small child.
Please do not forget us.
Where were you when the people
on the street facing your neighbors
could not find the trail?
The uncle who blew my flute
and gave me laughter always disappeared
without any promise of returning from
the middle of the Mediterranean.
The body of his lovely
three-year-old son was found
by survivors on a beach in Turkey.
Historical sites have been
erased as much as people.
There were times
when we looked at the moonlight
that began to fade and resolved the thirst
by receiving the rain from the sky
from time to time.
My nostalgic brothers will breathe on what earth.
Brothers, do not forget me.

Give me a breath.
When the dust embedded in the deep lung escape,
please fill the empty space with your breath.

2

For those who remain in the fertile land,
the voice of the protest for their freedom
still remains in our hearts.
See the rich harvests
from the city of that civilization.
No one has yielded under the violence,
and the fruit is bloomed by the remnant.
A few persons!
Do not forget the impression of that day
on the road to Damascus.
Someday when the sad stories of
the Mediterranean will come out again,
Oh! Here we will stand up again
and meet a new day.
Do not look into the sunset side.
In the day when the moonlight
of the night sky rises,
someday the dawn will come to dawn,
gathering the light and going along this long,
narrow path, strolling through the memories of
the day.

3

Aleppo, I wish I could dream of the future.
It is not a dream that is dominated
by despair, pain, and fear,
but a good dream of hope and recovery.
I'm waiting for the day
when all the guns still on the streets of Aleppo
disappear like morning mist.
On that day, we all will hold each other
and drink a toast together.
I will welcome the people who have left far away,
repair the fallen wall, walk down the dug road,
walk this way to the marching.
You will have to hear the sad story about
the camp built on the land of ashes
and comfort them.
No memory can dominate love.
Syria, a star floating on the universe!

Palestine

Those who went to the east,
those who walked across the barrier
with the word of hope, cannot meet now.
Does the Jubilee flower bloom there as well?
We must remember we were a brother.
We have to forget the fear of each other.
There must not forget the footsteps of the camels
who cross the wilderness path alone.
If you meet a distant oasis on the way,
give us a red ribbon for us on the rising spring.
We hope to be such a person as to hand
the bottled water to the thirsty.

2

We remember the memories of those days
in the old tent in the land where milk
and honey flowed and the stories
that are blooming in the battlefield.
As we walked along the long bank of the west,
I heard the children crying in the sand dust.
When will you have a nice face here?
The brethren who wanted to see will soon appear
at the entrance of the village
to be built again along this bank.
That day will come soon.

We'll see you as a bride
who will welcome the bridegroom.
We will make a bright flower corolla
and hang it on their neck and kiss your joy.
A shy virgin!
When you put your ears on a long barrier,
you will hear a small sound across from you,
and hopefully will always flow with your heart.

3

The day will come when all things
around will be restored.
Until then,
we must endure the day's fear and despair.
Without a day of joy,
we would not stand for a moment.
We need to know that the patience
we need is no longer luxury.
The long shadows of those who cross
the desert on a stallion stud begin to be seen.
It's about the time when the dusk will be long.
It has not been dark yet.
The wind that urges time does not blow either.
At the border, everything around you is still.
I will listen to the shouts of
those who are in my ears
and wait silently for
when this tabernacle is being harvested.

Korea

A place where no one came
for half a century
Heaven and earth meet and marry.
After giving birth it gave birth
to a child on the earth.
The river is blocked
Mountains blocked
It has been split
since the broken Baekdudaegan's spirit
and gave birth to a deformed child.
They are called Siamese-twins.
Without seeing each other's faces
The close-filled scarf skin came into
each other's blood.
When one cries, one wipes the tears.
If one of you is sick,
Although the body is attached to two
One must die before the other lives.
Attached to the back
When the thorns come one by one,
Distant future
Here,
the two of us will be holding hands together
and running side by side.
Like a disease that does not have
to die anymore

when it's time to lighten up...

2

We want to see who's going to end
this long farewell,
the faces of those who we've missed
before the sun goes over that.
We are afraid that all those memories
that will be easily forgotten
until then will disappear.
When you call the names of your brothers,
the only thing that comes back
is the cry of the goose
that goes beyond the barbed wire.

Japan

It was once born on land.
You forget the smell of fresh grass.
You miss the smell of moist soil,
You've been following
the road a number of times
but you can not see it.
It is now an island that can not return,
a country of dead souls that are isolated.

2

We remember the brutal tyranny
of the summer that was hot.
Through the frenzied appearance of the grieving
and rejoicing of all the poor
as they go out begging for the day's life,
I watched the pictures of the hungry children
who could not fill even if they filled it.
Have you seen a cloud sitting
on a mountain beyond?
I know the mountains
that can not be surrendered,
the place where it stays,
the trails that are scattered,
the trails of Hikikomori
that followed the long journeys of rich,

but never happy children
The morning of the mine
has always started
with a fuzzy black dust.

3

When have you ever seen
cherry blossoms in the spring?
The flower buds of the garden
have not woken up yet.
Little birds that did not feel spring
in the northern wind
could not nest on tree branches.
Branches resemble your souls.
Trees that do not bear fruit are now desolate
dried branches.
Will spring come in your arms?
Birds that do not have their nests fly
in the cruel season.
A lord leaves a long way
and does not know when to return,
the ferocious aura that robbed his master drove
the flowering spring.
When have you ever seen cherry blossoms
in the spring?
Have you ever seen birds
that crossed the river of death to a desolate land?

4

There was a stranger
who walked a far mountain road.
For him, there was only one cane
that could survive
only one meal and tiredness.
The moonlight swept him away,
and the sun did not shine on him.
When people met him on the road,
they drove away in a different way
without greeting.
The stranger was so lonely,
he tried to be friends with the deer
from the mountain,
the deer began to flee as soon as it saw him
from afar.
On the sea became a lonely island,
in the night sky it became a falling meteor,
only a bag and a bottle of
water remained to him,
which could not hold anything.
Friend! Before leaving a long way,
you had such a splendid life!
Do not you regret it?
The fact that past years have deceived you so far,
if you had not resembled anything,
there would be a little compassion toward you,
it is indeed pitiful that you walk alone

on a dark and scary mountain path.

5

I do not expect to get up again
because you have strength on your lying legs.
Now that you will be tired,
it is time to lay down and sleep.
I hope you will be waiting for
an unexpected guest
when you sit on a bench
in a waiting room
in a small station of countryside
until you hear horn sound of train
in your dreams.
Do not forget that when the yellow ginkgo trees
in front of the station change the colors,
the autumn will end and the long winter will
come.

China

Look at that active volcano
that burns red and boils down!
The ground was not ready to welcome them.
It was a remembrance of the cruel heat
and the lost orphanage of the red earth.
Where have the priests of the east
who ran on the back of the beast,
the warriors of the field
who had eaten the old iron,
and the saints who had been driven
out of the armies of revolution
and gone to the Gobi Desert?
Tears of compassion, fist clenched,
sons of the wind
sleeping in bamboo forests,
blinding eyes to dancing across the border.
The direction of the flowing lava can not be determined.
The sea has become too desolate to accept,
and the earth is not mature.
The towns of the dragons flapping out,
the deep sleep has always been a horror to us.
We met people on the street
who do not love people.
I met an active volcano there.

2

The foxes of the desert
which dwell in the dust will soon collapse
and dig into their holes to become sand-graves.
In a bizarre form that changes thousands of
times a night,
it loses its image
and dreams of memories in there.
They crossed the continent.
They set the boundaries of countless horizons,
and inscribed it on rocks that would not be
erased even in strong winds.
The revolution was just a fantasy,
and soon greed was brought to bed.
They regret knowing
that desert was their home
and friend and lover.
It was the moment
when thousands of years
of buried treasure were revealed.
There were neither guests,
great revolutionaries nor
poets crying out for freedom.
What remains for those obsessed with the border
is just one unknown fence ...,

3

You have a strong heart
that does not look at the weak.
Can not you hear the roar of the earth
and the swallowing of people?
Where did they go along
the distant Silk Road to your friends
who crossed the river
and climbed the mountain of death?
In the fallen ideology and the sinking belief,
you wake up from the last sleep
and form a huge mountain,
but only the fierce coldness
and loneliness on there.
The 12 animals suffering
from the pain of hunger
and growth every day,
and the ones without the owner,
hear only the silent sound of the wind.
If you are in the middle of the world,
where the cold season is always there
without the last sympathy for the dying weak,
stay in the center of warmth.
Teach them to live together, not alone.
Remember the letters of your friends long ago.
Let everybody know that the Yangtze River
was not always grayish.

4

The wall built across the continent resembles
the mind and heart of a stranger.
The persons who came to the stars
in faraway universe,
buried their dreams in the loamy earth to
achieve civilization
and become our faraway empire.
A less mature child who has lost
his pure emotion
can not sleep at night with fear
and fear of losing his parents,
crossing the desert barefoot, climbing the rock,
crossing the long river,
and sleeping in a civilized world.
You could not close the door of the long fence
because you could not find the red bird
that had disappeared
into the field reed forest
after leaving the side long
after the life that became the fantasy.
Can dancers dancing on the wall fall into fossils,
and when the kings
and the warriors who lost their palaces
become ordinary people
and can not find their traces,
can they find their hearts and their spirits?
It was the princes of civilization

who could not even see the people
who pile up to the edge of the earth
and build up the wall.

5

They were the ones who came up to the depths
of the inland through
the distant sea looking for origin.
They made pottery, breathed into the soil,
peeled thin mucous membranes,
and received the light.
Then they soon forgot their origins
and wandered again
for thousands of years.
They said that they were the king of the east,
and they chased the waterway to go from the
outskirts to the center.
Sometimes they tried to climb over the fog
and ride thousands of high mountain peaks
on the back of the phoenix.
In the desire to threaten
the small mountains surrounding them
and to lead to a mountain range,
they repeatedly stumbled over
with an obsessive desire to find origin
and anger against one another.
Ah! Do not stand in the center.
Do not try to change the flowing water.

Time is already on your back,
and when you humbly accept
those who are left as mercy
and tolerance as the majesty of a prince,
you will be restored to its original form
and all the days that have passed.

India

Your temperament resembles
the white cotton of a soft cotton field.
Equatorial country,
gathered in the Plaza of
the peace song of equality
and popular resistance
in the brown chapleted saints of Orient,
a country that is alive and well off, old,
the country that ignores the old colonies,
the neglected and turning away
from class to stand tall as
a country calling for freedom.
The people of the square!
August under a scorching sun of great men
and women who loved!
A confession in front of the chastity
and all lift up and down the walls survive
pass onto the cusp of history by starlight of
Orient back now
and in front of his aged parents.
Now you are a young man in front of old parents.
It was the appearance of our children.

2

People stood on countless stairs.

The long silent pilgrimage from the highest
to the lowest tired of the brown people,
sprinkled with lye on mountains and rivers
that could not reach into the sky,
closed the door of wisdom
and looked like a long traveler to death.
The white veterans refused to lie down
in their coffins,
and they tried to enter the universe
as part of nature.
It was the march of the lost stars.
Wisdom was a wanderer who dug wells
that did not come out of the water,
people on the stairs,
people who lived in the caves of Hermit.
Ignorance does not blossom.
Rolls rocks toward the top of the mountain
and makes stairs.
It was a secret city, artificial garden,
gorgeous night of festivals,
and in the morning
we saw people sleeping tired every street.

3

The breeze blew. It was a gentle breeze
suitable for grazing. In the woods,
the pride of Asia Tigers of Bengal also fell asleep
in the warmth and tranquility of the wind.

The forest seemed to guard the earth's
conscience.
It turned back the clock of civilization,
and it was their ministry that no human
intelligence could make.
When the deep silence wakes up,
this place will take a short trip back
to the old days of glory.
Was it a beautiful girl? One day,
when the inequality for man
and the day of class collapses,
and the true shape can be found,
this forest will be full of fresh green fragrance.
It will be an oasis when the shadows of desire are
all disappeared,
and the day to go is still far away.
Do not change the milestones.
Populace in the forest!

4

The investigators living in the forest,
"Are you looking for a way?"
Do not come this way.
A long time ago, many goers left the road
in the road and left.
When the dust ran up,
people woke up in the middle of Asia
and tried to go home,

but the wind stopped them.
The clouds taught them the wrong direction.
In a few hundred years,
there was a time when we lost consciousness
while receiving the rude title of another nation.
Meet the people who still live in the mountains.
When the seasons change
and the leaf is renewed again
in the borehole tree,
the road in the path will be revealed.
Then the day will come again.

5

In the red ocher of the Ganga river,
I saw people picking up life.
The consciousness of sending
and receiving would have washed away
the moments of joy that had sought the way,
the people who wanted to be sublime,
and the dark rivers would have gone back
to their original days of innocence.
They dance with cloth every hand.
Birds in noble dreams also resolve thirst
in the river.
I saw a sculpture of an elephant
whose throat was cut there.
People were washed from the sculpture
and drunk water

that flows down to the river
and arranged their lives.
Someday,
waiting for the days to be called, leaving the
river, and eventually returning to the place,
all of them washed their bodies by washing their
mouths with a loincloth.
Have we ever been conscious of life like them?
Have you ever bent your back humbly?
It seemed now that I knew
that the colors of the tree
and grass on the river were so beautiful.

Mongolia

I saw people wandering
in the vast grasslands.
In the center of the world,
they embraced the green land of blessings
that reached the sky.
It is a huge square of the earth,
once the center of all the discussions,
the hermit land of those who now live in
silence and compromise,
the flying eagle crowd,
the resemblance of the mighty wild horses
running through the ground,
through the frozen land of the north to
Americas,
then, through Europe and the Middle East,
they revealed the fire of the square.
The day will come when the people
who sleep in the fields wake up
and look for their roots.
The day will come when the fire
comes back on the square,
and the people who will hold
the earth again will be here.

2

They had the fastest horses
in the world running across the field.
In the tireless courage and passion,
all the countries of the world relied on your news.
Genghis Khan,
the empire with the largest territory,
the country that opened
the doors of east-west exchanges
in the center of the era,
although now the territory is divided
and the kingdom is ended and weakened,
but the traces of your great history
will be here for a long time,
Let's survive in a spirit that
does not collapse like comets coming,
and let us know the cycle of history strictly
in future generations.
Leave the eternal and great earthly empire
clearly marked on the stone
that there is no one left and can not rule.
The plaza of the continent!
Teachings flowing in the wind!

3

There I heard a whisper in the wind.
There was freedom from obsession to have a lot.

And I knew what the beauty of obedience was
in the big eyes of the nomadic livestock.
The guests from the desert across
the prairie were literally tinged,
and the whisper dripped the dried ground
with the rain of wisdom
and abundance by teaching
and enlightenment.
Did you see the colors that riding on horseback?
 It was the hill of the warriors of yellow,
blue,
white,
black
and red, and the color of the glorious days.
They embellished the world.
And now he has turned back to the far
and became the land of the silent people.
 It became the origin of the earth.

Philippines

The rich gifts you had
and the beautiful sea shadows of turquoise
did not become a great comfort to
those sick days.
You went to the ocean with a wide heart,
as if holding a summer typhoon in your arms.
Looking at the moonlight
floating on the surface of the water,
you awoke your sleeping mind with a big cry
over 7107 firm shoulders.
A poor people's kingdom,
a treasure island stuck in the sea, wake up
and go back to the blue ocean.
The people's life will rise again on that day,
as the palm trees in the beach forest dare to
climb up the harbor of the world
with a sublime mind that can not climb daringly.
Become a port of the earth
resembling a shining emerald.
Do not go back to the life of submission,
but to a country
where the people have become masters,
revive with the undivided lungs that flow clear
air into the heart!
7107 breathing cells!

2

The stones that were raised against
you did not break your hard heart
and the crust.
Your innumerable efforts to escape bondage
were like the days
when you had your passion like a hot fire
and resembled a long gesture.
When we hear a huge trumpet like
an active volcano,
we awaken from a deep sleep
and head back to the ocean.
The bitter roots of some dictatorship
that will stop you
will now disappear like fogs scattered in the sea
in front of stern populace and past blue youths.
A country where the sunlight does not always
disappear!
Break down the chain of all bondage
and stand on the same country
as your mother who feeds babies.
Then we hear the sound of your breathing cells.
Dance on the sea to the sound of
passionate music.
Whenever you break an idol
and sprinkle it with ashes,
the new spring will come again.

With youthful ardor,
be burning and reborn
to go back to your place
where we met with light steps.

3

Will all the chains of oppression
and fear ever break?
And when is the day when the liberated citizens
will pour out into the streets?
Look at the cathedral built
on this land a long time ago.
All the false prophets who ignore
the spirit of the people
and abstain from power are all leaving,
and when the crowd of young pilgrims
who are about to go the right way is now full,
they will lightly fly like butterflies,
There are memories of young people
on beautiful beaches,
and people share their love heartly.
The island of passion!
Blow with the hearts of the people!

Indonesia

I still can not forget the tears in your eyes.
Like the pearls poured down like a meteor,
and still waiting for those who love,
you have retained the splendor of primitive.
Do not forget. In the jungle where the tears are
washed away like jewels
that still shine like pearls,
and the heart beats louder,
we find those who love again here
That there will be a day
to come back to the woman,
that the pain of her parturition
is only momentary,
If you remember the words of the teacher
who always said
that you should not go the wrong way,
remembering the tears of God.
you will know where your future will wait for
you.

2

When all the things of the past summer raised
one by one in our minds,
We saw brave trees that
were not shaken in the typhoon, but

were firmly rooted and kept their fruits.
Today we will see beautiful forests
like the lungs of this earth,
just as we were hanging on tens of thousands
of non-falling branches
and shining the last glistening fruits,
Those who steal this beautiful face
will go into deep waters
with typhoons,
and when the birds twitter and the feast
on the abundant table are restored,
the watchmen guarding the forest
will return one by one.
The hot sunshine of a day
will not reach your enthusiasm,
it will always be a green spring for our girls
who wear makeup and colorful clothes.

Sri Lanka

I met a woman on the street.
On the far peninsula,
I saw the beautiful woman who was preparing
for the last farewell from the place
where she was staying for a while.
There may be waiting times for the people
who are waiting for peace,
holding the people to wipe her tear,
protecting the treasures like pearls,
and the festivals that convey
the joys of liberation
and the oppressed. Now we have to get up.
People who hold plows and hoes in their hands!
Sit on the east side and watch the rising sun.
Peel off the time of old customs,
roll out idols like heavy stones,
go out into the jungle
where the tiger roars out of the cave
and wipe away the tears of a woman
sitting on the street.
She will reach out for reconciliation.
You will not be tears of a peninsula,
but a jewel like a pearl.
On that day everyone would be together,

2

When it rained to announce
the resurrection of the ruined farm,
all the silent people went to the loamy earth.
The fragrance of tea that perches
at the tip of the tongue makes you
forget the days of farms that were deserted.
When the seasons come,
when people come to dance on them,
to defeat the temptations,
and to bloom again,
they will see here again those who return home.
Take off the idols of the rouge.
And in the midst of pain and courage of pearls,
set aside on the sea, and let people know
that your presence is firmly alive in oppression.
The meditators from the savanna pastures!

PART 2

Myanmar

I met a nomadic man in a high mountain
near the sky.
Tears in the eyes became dew
in the midst of the mountains at dawn,
and for a time there was a mountain temple
that people could not live in.
The human abyss became valleys
where water did not flow,
and they resembled the heart of an orphan,
who had been forsaken
in the millennial kingdom,
and they went into deeper caves
and became murals.
Their voices were not heard on the mount.
The child monks abandoned alone
in dictatorship,
see the wandering souls who entered
the wrong path,
without knowing how to abandon the pain
during the silent ascetic practices in a mountain.
Hate conceived Na raka, the infernal regions.
I met people with long paraphasia there and
listened to a deep cry.
Every night,
the moon of revenge came up
from the top of the mountain,

and the ghosts of each other,
which can not be broken,
turned into fire every day,
making the ruined place once lush.
It was a garden of sorrow
and I saw a dry valley where no water flowed.

2

At least the awe and courtesy for purity
and nature should not be lost.
Don't forget that someday
We'll be one of the consequences
of what we have to do,
and we'll hear from our children
who don't know the names
and waiting for their parents.
We should see our welcome
in the faintest birds of the forest
and in the innocent eye of mountain beasts
we meet on the mountain road by chance.
They must be aware of their sadness
that they can not guard against human beings
and fail to keep even their limited areas.
Look at the way you walk.
The people of the forest, that the roads
were never made without small or large stones!
Do not burn the fragrance of death.

Vietnam

The descendants of the peninsula,
with its beautiful, deep-sounding copper lines,
have survived for thousands of years,
but have been robust and vitality.
The rich paddy field was similar
to the strong hand
of her mother to feed the strangers
of the hungry earth.
Where are the warriors
with copper-skinned skin
in the toughest bonds that can not be broken?
Break the chain tied to the two legs
and stand back to the land of the true populace.
On the day when the monsoon
was blowing and it rained a lot,
I saw the women standing
on the Mekong River and wearing Ao dai.
I watched them live, resisting in the ocherous
water flowing down the river.
Whenever we feel thirst,
their territory is like undried wells.
Ao dai woman!
Walk the road! Sing your song,
awaken those who are asleep,
soak your throat with a cupful of tea and awaken
your consciousness.

2

Just like you have gone to the wrong way
on the mountain for a while,
now you have to climb to a high place
to look at your current location.
One day he will come in the clouds
and clothe with white clothes,
and give him the milk and honey
that is hungry for the land.
See those who have been shed
in the blood of your land.
Was not it because of the resistance
of the wretched peninsula,
that it did not survive
in a formidable oppression and deprivation?
I went down the valley
where the water between the mountains flows.
In front of the spectacular sight,
I saw your future.
It boasts a vast mountain range,
a place like your heart filled
with infinite treasures,
the homeland of unspoiled people,
and now a dazzling figure like a growing boy.

3

Numerous people have disappeared

as dust in places where there is no one
across the border.
Indexed names that are still inkless
on white paper,
inaccessible hearings and signals
in the distant universe,
and breathless creatures have become fossils
in the caves of any mountain.
I saw the ruins of idols in their secret places,
and I saw people dancing in joy all night
as the blue moon waited for dawn,
disappearing over the mountains.

Cambodia

There is a sound of your wailing
all over the land of dark-red color.
Those who are still in the deep underworld
and can not come to the world of light!
There is no one on the isolated island
that is silent in front of the relics of the gods to
come and face each other.
There is no forerunner to watch over tyranny
and oppression over the moonless sky.
Those who left the road a long time ago,
without promise to return,
the remaining widows tear down
the dripping water falling
from the bamboo house without the owner
and endlessly flowed to the river,
and the dreams of the children
began to grow deep in the river.
We should now finish their story.
But there is no one to listen to.
In a place where you can not hear sounds
from far away,
only the strange birds
and the wind were the masters.

2

Do not be afraid of the future,
do not be sad or despair of past.
We are now looking for a way
on a street in Phnom Penh.
The way to the temple of oblivion,
everyone is gathering both hands,
calling the names of those
who are not in this world, marching.
You have endured the monsoon climate and saw
that you tried to overcome with silence
like a faded murals.
Mekong's strength and softness make
you build up again.
On that day, the shackles tied to
your ankles are released,
waiting for the moment when you will return to
your mother's back in the forest.
We learned how to endure sadness through you.
As we gaze at the many shadows
that lie on the streets,
we are drawing a picture of yourself flying freely
as a small bird is released.

Laos

The road to Phu Bia was not that steep and far.
It is because we met the gentle
and hearted people on the trip
and worked together.
The sun that falls to the west is a place
where it rests for a while.
It is like a sister's bosom.
It embraces the heaven
and earth with both hands
and waits for a quiet revolution.
In that deep mountain,
the cries and resistance of
the good people are still heard.
We became friends on.
In the thirst of dryness,
when the water flowing in the valleys was lifted,
it became a friendship of the guest
which had become a cloud
in the midst of the mountain.
They have never been poor.
They always knew how to learn satisfaction in
their simple dining table.
Now that the owner of
this land is not one of them,
 take off your old clothes
and decorate them nicely.

2

We will always remember the day.
On the day when all things go back
to their place,
the day when a small red bird crying,
lost in the deep mountains,
and crying for his mother's bosom,
goes back to her house and finds a peaceful day,
You will not forget your name engraved on it,
your brilliant appearances of thousands of years
of constantly changing new clothes.
The people of Lao,
I saw a spring day with sprouting over your
shoulders wearing dyed clothes and dancing.

3

Where we can hear
all the sounds of the earth,
quietly we close our eyes
and we are always there.
The hope for the future
that will emerge in the depths
below the strata will be able to flourish again
on all your ruined forms.
So we are going our way together.

Tibet

The great product of creation,
the high mountains,
created the boundaries beneath the universe.
The indomitable warriors
who constantly rise again
without bowing to the threats
of the northern barbarians
and their fears,
the hearts of the innocent surviving
in silent silence
resemble the highest peaks.
Everyone was a friend in the way
that met the meditators from all sides.
The sound of horse hooves
running in the blue, red, green,
and yellow winds of thousands of miles is filled
with bravery, purity, richness, peace and
kindness.
When I looked at the land with the bright eyes of
an eagle rising above the sky,
I could always find
the hidden meaning of weakness
in the strength of strength in weakness.

2

You are going to leave
for seeking the peace of mind
in the nature of this plains.
Every foot you walk in
is engraved with stories of millions of people
who have passed through this ancient place.
You have stood the time with a strong heart,
and now you know what pleasure it is
to conform to time and nature,
like a handful of ashes in the wind.
It was a place where human greed could not reach.

Bhutan

We are standing in front of a land
that is quietly silent with a mysterious figure
that is enveloped by dawn mist and dew,
and resembles a strong tendon
that accepts everything
without any greed for given things.
You have many things that we do not have.
We must remember that mind.
We look at a young yak that climbs
through a steep and fertile valley.
The kingdom from the top of
the mountain was always there.
Where is your heart
and the way you want to go?
Now we are standing in a sapphire land
where we dress and enjoy fine clothes.
As a child,
we would like to have old tales nightly
while taking off our mysterious veil
as we met our friend who played in the alley.
Let's climb this mountain together.
New friends will be waiting there.
You will see a beautifully created world.

2

You have ome from a distance in time,
and have become one heart
in the very center of the earth.
The footsteps left behind are filled with
the sounds of familiar scent and joy,
resting on the minds of those
who are going to rest
for a while with the songs of the forest.
One night the meteors were pouring,
we left together.
The fragrance was buried on a tree branch
so that it would not be lost again.
Do not forget that day,
let's get ready when someone comes to us.
Let's wait for someone to hold the light and
breathe the breath of life.

Nepal

Do not forget the time
you were filled with sorrow.
Today, there was a drizzle
all night in the mountain.
The morning sun will rise
and wait for the day full of light.
When was the day? Learn tolerance,
bury the spirit of wood, stone,
and iron in the wet ground,
and search for new paths with the survivors.
In the distant future, a person will come.
A young man who lived on
this land thousands of years before
he remembered beauty will
come up in the white clouds,
and again in this bare garden
it will grow with colorful flowers
and various fruit trees,
and clear water will flow
down the mountain again.
Until then, you must remember this garden.
You must wipe our tears and stand up again.
My brothers!

2

In the brown continent
we always looked for a person.
Like a tranquil lake, in the summer
I was looking for a naive person to stay
for a while and to celebrate.
Let's remember when we had a toast together.
Do not forget the donkeys
and the farmer's innocent smile
that have been poor but always diligent
and have climbed the mountain trail.
I just went out to find a man with a wide heart
that would shake hands to the flowers
that we did not even see.
The man who did not know where to wait for us,
and looked up into the sky
and saw migratory birds over the high
Himalayas.

Bangladesh

Did you see that many falling stars?
we saw the last images of children with sad eyes,
on the streets, staring at the sky,
and the children of the earth saddened
by hunger, abuse, and sorrow.
Where should they go?
The roads were blocked,
and the houses built with red bricks collapsed
and lost their ground.
Where are the gods you believe and follow?
Memories are all buried deep in the ground.
Do not forget the way back
you used to run away barefoot
on an abandoned ground
like an orphan and a widow.
Can you pick up those stars that are always
scattered on the red land?
In the collapsed city,
we waited for the day to rise again,
bowed down,
and today we went to a busy street.
we saw it there.
Was the people's crust and gaze so cold?
we saw stars falling in the polluted river
that no one gave them.

Again, those clear stars that will be brought back to someone.

2

**People began to abandon this street.
And they began to travel to a distant country.
Someday when their hopes come on again,
this street will have a quiet morning again.
Even today, people started to ride the train.
And cross the river dozens of times a day
to negotiate a distant future.
As the train passed, a dusty wind blew.
Inside, the people disappeared again,
and the tears of Dhaka flowed over the shoulders.**

Malaysia

You look like a little tiger lying
in the bosom of nature.
I fell asleep to feel peace in the calm bosom.
When I stayed overnight in Kinabalu,
I saw the only friends who came to.
I watched a child's sleeping in their arms
and the dream of an Aboriginal
who ran through the jungle.
Is not it beautiful?
Today I walk in the middle of this mountain,
looking down the ground
on a hillside for a while,
and I knew that someday
there will come true peace.
Remember that day.
Maybe the day will take off all the shells,

2

Over a thousand years,
you had a brilliant dream on the land,
dreams of the nation and the countless people
who died in the land and who built it.
On the day when the stories of the poor people
who refused colonization
and came out into the streets flowed

from children's lips,
there was one.
They picked up the falling petals
and made the wreaths .
 Do not they look like the skirt of a shy virgin?
Someday there will meet the natives
from the east.
Let go of all the vanity and wisdom,
 and dream in the three rivers flowing
into the sea.
Would not you like to find out
what the most valuable thing looks like holding
treasure in your arms?

Taiwan

The Island of Liberty,
floating alone in the Pacific Ocean,
sees an island of emptiness
quietly gathering hands
that yearn for liberation
and peace at the end of the territory it sees.
Their soul is indeed precious.
It is a land of humanity
that never seems small.
It was the first breakwater
we met at the epicenter of the typhoon,
the last shelter of those
who drift down to the sea,
the future always begins there
and ends with an ancient roots!
Keep your precious artifacts
and do not forget to shout
for freedom and democracy!
Let them never know
that suffering can not win injustice!
We heard the midnight storm
and thunder that stayed there.
On the day when it falls to the ground without end,
the island that has been heated by the passion
will wake up again,

and the touch of it will touch the sleeping one.
Home and Nation of the people!
A nest of pure souls not tempted by the specter!

2

In the face of numerous rulers and oppression,
there was a strong spirit that never bent.
We saw it with our eyes today.
Let's call the names of friends
who have forgotten all their false imaginations,
wonders and gloomy times and miss their
hometown.
The spring sun was always warm,
and the summer typhoon was not that scary.
In there, Aboriginal Breathe.
When the simple nostalgic passions
that are now alive through the vast aspirations
that are alive and ready to rise again
will have the oval space always running in
parallel,
you will be alive with a heart that is always lush
and mild.

Singapore

It was a city where you can see
the sun rise and fall.
We were able to count
the hours of the day in busy seas
where there was abundance and agitation
and we could bump into
to greet people at the harbor.
What do you think? Toward that sea, little boy!
Look back at those days
of embracing the continent
and having the ocean in your youth
and infinite imagination.
Do ask your passions in the streets to feel
the hot heat of summer like a friendly
friend you met in the equator
and to rise again in the heavy oppression
and bridle that you lost in all your life.
It was always people's part.
In this well-organized city
we dream of a primitive jungle.
Young men and women of the equator
that simplicity,
 temperance, and refined times are not in vain!

2

We should not always forget the old days.
The remnants of a storm in the sea
that night was so scary.
Remember that you can come back
to this land anytime.
Listen to the shouts of the poor.
That those who persecute them
can not stand up again.
It must be declared before the law of nature.
It is not a faint future like
the fog of the disappearing sea.
On that day we will come back here again,
young man!
we will change clothes made of colored fabrics,
stand there with a light footstep,

Hong Kong

We spent the night in Macau.
The remaining hours of the night invited
the dead of the old garden,
and the strange clock tower's hour hand
pointed to 1 am.
Was the shadows made from the lamps
of the other side of the building
looking like the walls
of the gray gardens
were the warriors of gorgeous civilizations?
As we can not see again,
we have seen the port of the continent
that took our sight away,
old homeless people lost there,
and the soulless people seeking their way
through their shadows.
Looking at the mysticists and ancient relics
that preceded the times,
the smoke and smell that rose
from the priestless temple did not leave the city.
It is a place where the east and the west meet,
where the dew is quietly blossomed,
the girl waiting for the spring,
can always meet and talk about the memories of
the old days,

Thailand

Chao Phraya,
along the river that started from the rainforest,
tells a good story of people
and a whisper about good days.
Looking at the old carved stones
as much as the history of the place
in the middle of the temple,
I saw the strong and colorful festivals
that can not be cleared of the traces
of the depths engraved on human hearts.
Still, there are still good people living in
denying civilizations in the primeval forests.
There is a spirit of resistance against the smell
and domination of the woman who met at the
foot of the mountain.
She danced towards the mountain.
The figure crossed the ridge in one line.
Everyone who met along
the Long River gave pleasure,
righteousness, and simplicity.
We walked along the line there.
When you grab this line,
which seems to lead somewhere,
there will be a road that has never been there
before.

2

We met a man who made poetry
and sang in Chiang Mai all over the world.
earnest young man!
I hope your song will continue
until those days are over.
He is going to repair
and rebuild the ruined place.
It's an early hour for the night to come here.
The noon sun will continue to stay here.
Until that time,
we will collect the scattered birds
singing on this stoned road.
The moment will come
when the dust will be clean.
Look at your creation.
It will become a vessel to contain all the universe,
and it will come to dance with shouting together.
A new day will come. Together, let's head for the day.

3

I miss young people. Look at their fists.
Listen to their cries that survive in the high, fertile mountains
and stretch out into the mighty skies.

**Scary storms give way to them
by bowing their heads in front of them.
When you hold your hand,
you can feel the touch of a rough,
hardened hand. In a strong form,
the land mixed with pebbles
and stones will become lofty,
and the land will produce commodities.
Let's not forget to pick up
the fallen ears in the fall.
In order not to forget our hunger days,**

Pakistan

I stood on a land full of fragrance of Jasminum
and looked at the moonlight disappearing.
On a day when a man's fondness
for the past was heard,
and the sound of a shepherd's flute
ringing in a serene mountain,
the small animals of the forest lay down together
and counted the stars that were in the sky.
There will be signs of salvation
on this earth as well.
For those who are forsaken,
those beautiful days to find the house again
and take it in the arms of the family.
I watched the Indus river
from Karakouram highway.
How many stories are contained
in that stream downstream?
I saw the future of this land in the shrewd
but strong form of the crowd of Markhor
who came down to the river that night and
celebrated the night.
Do not go in the wrong direction.
Little warriors,
Do not forget that the shepherd
is still looking for you
in the place where you have left.

Kazakhstan

The Aral Sea, the sea of the islands
of the Asian continent,
the plateau of the vast earth, the Caspian Sea,
the clear and damp morning dew
that began in the country of silence
drains the vast heat of the earth.
Today we hold our hands
and climb up this mountain
and tell the sound they tell.
A refined rhythm that resonates deeply calls
the name of a traveler
who sleeps in a deep unconsciousness.
Beautiful epic!
See the people standing in front of
the center of the square
following the wanderer and standing as an
independent of this life.
We learned that the path was not in vain,
but through the life of
a small good man in Astana.
The merchants of the streets, too,
were amazed at the beauty of the veiled woman.
We will wait for those brilliant days to stand
as an independent when people
in white clothes follow
the purity of lilies and sing songs

with us on the streets.

2

On the day when clear water
flows back to Syr Darya,
the thirsty with this place will be gone,
and it will be the day of singing
the song of liberation,
and the Gentiles who came from
a distant country
will wait for us to drink this water.
On that day all unclean and dirty clothes
will be taken off and ready to be changed.
Together, when we see the rising sun
in the high garden,
the sorrow will pass away,
and the sunrise clouds will come to this land.

Afghanistan

Have you seen a camel lost in the desert?
Strangers from faraway places,
never been rich and happy.
There was neither a winner nor a loser
in the place where the dew falling
at dawn dried up
and only the hoarse of the young child
who lost his parents on the dry land
where the snowy breeze covering
the last winter's land
could be felt could be heard.
We follow the memories in the old brain
and follow their backs.
The dead in the desert,
the little foxes living in the rock crevices
are alone
without friends. Where have they gone?
The wrinkled face of the old woman
who waits for a son to return to the war,
the stories of Kabul who lost time,
the people who lost a shepherd,
the faces of the desert waiting
for the morning of recovery,

2

You have to forget everything.
Here are the memories, sorrows
and fears of Kabul.
The city was destroyed and the inhabitants
crossed the Mediterranean to Europe.
You'll see trees, grasses and flowers
that you've seen anywhere in there.
When will you return to dry land.
When the stories of the hometowns
on the wind and the laughter of
the vanished people are heard,
when one returns to
an unrestrained land of peace,
people will wait there.
When the cold winter passes,
and there is no shaking of the earth,
will spring come here?
Will the days of long wandering come to finish?

Uzbekistan

Tashkent,
I walked over a dry desert without water.
The rain from the summer sky disappeared
before reaching the ground,
and the names of the people there began to erase
one by one in the sandstorms of the desert.
Was it late summer when light-colored weeds
began to grow with cracked hands?
By the time the night seemed so short,
I met the Sage from the East
and talked all night.
Tender stories such as soft cotton
became the stars of the night sky
and shared a long dream along
the Silk Road with a long time friend
who dreamed for the independence.
Like a dry rain, catching
the future for the moment,
we hold the wrist of the little boy
who forgot the days and stands on the two rivers.

2

Now we have to send people.
You must know the sadness of
little unnamed birds

flapping on the palm and escaping
and read the moonlight's mind
floating on the solitary lake alone.
How many people shed tears here
and bid farewell,
the generation dreaming of the future?
We will listen to and remember
the myriad stories of Samarqand
and and be engraved in the hearts of
those who remember
and cross the river across the mountain.
Do not forget that there are still a lot of people
waiting to read and tell their stories.

3

Minorities are sad,
but one should not forget that the season
is coming to an end someday.
At that time, it will be pleased
with the cherry blossoms
in front of the plaza and
will release the buds first.
Take comfort in this wide square with the poor.
When we go to a corner of a marginalized street
and call a friend's name,
they sing a song of liberation with everyone.
If it was a sunny day after it rained,
if it was a sunny day,

Kyrgyzstan

Manas,
on the Day of the unbelievable revolution,
which is not yielded,
on the mountain which rose high.
A fountain that never drains will be in the land,
awakening a sleeping ritual to the clear sound of
pure children ringing at the foot of a mountain,
in a quiet village.
We went to Lake Issyk-Kul once.
I knew from there that the land had not dried
for long and made a clear spring water.
Look at the sun rising over the mysterious
and glittering color water surface.
There are still those who are not
unrighteous in this place,
and when they hear the music of the grasslands,
they will wake up and enter the deep mountains
to meet the splendid season.

2

You should not get used to darkness anymore.
No one will find anyone that night.
In the busy hands of a tiny little clown,
people mistook reality for their dreams
and forgot the city.

And they built their houses here,
not in cities, and became trees, stones, mountains,
and lakes. Everyone gets to dream at Ala Archa.
A single eagle flies into
the clouds over the mountain tops
and crosses the border.
It will return to this place without getting lost.
It was so beautiful and brilliant
that they did not forget their days.

3

We always dream of that day.
We gather and run out of the mountain
without any shortage,
and we dream of a day when we drink together
with clear water to the deep lake.
There is no quiet wind.
There is no passing by without all the shaking.
People with simple copper-skinned skin,
come out in bright colors.
And on that day when we stand in the middle,
our dreams will blossom together.

Tajikistan

We must cross that the Pamirs before sunset.
We have to find the gate of Silk Road
in a deep blue field.
We should look to the east where the sun rises.
Many have gone there
and have not heard of their news yet.
In this quiet plateau we held all the sounds
and meditated for a moment.
The soul is enough to capture nature,
and the climate of the desert is diminished.
We should follow the boy
with a small whip holding
his hand in the sound of the camel's bell.

2

There is a golden crown on your head.
When the stars of gold are shining
in the night sky,
Dushanbe prepares for a quiet morning.
In the midst of a deep contemplation
rise up in the tomb.
In that day, you should wake up
the sleepers of the city
with golden diadems and clothing.
The day will soon come when you will put

on the full scent of tulips
and your colored garments.
The breeze becomes our friend,
and we are comforted by the tired body
in the face of the shepherd descending from
the top of the mountain.
Your boldness and strength
must be firmly established.
Shepherd!
Let's go down this mountain together
and wake up the people of the quiet city there
and help rebuild this place.
For the future of Tajikistan,

Turkmenistan

Even in the depths of the earth,
no one came to meet
this quiet continent in the desert.
Do you see the far reaches of the Capet
Mountains?
It's where the hot heat of
summer goes to sleep.
In the thirsty sea we have
to find a way to Amu Darya.
For a moment,
we should cool off the heat of the day
in this desert oasis, share their old stories
that sometimes come from eating wild vines
and walnut fruit from the mountains
under cool shade.
Someday migratory birds will come here.
We will talk with all the good-hearted people
who live on quiet time in this well-made land,
like the old courtyard built in the history of
thousands of years,
watching the stars rising from the desert all
night long.

2

How many abyss are you talking about

in that picture sitting up from the pit?
We will never fail to
make a firm determination
that we should not lose our way
on the ground again.
Our destination was not much left.
The brothers will not cry again in the
underworld.
When the soul is comforted
and the one who can deliver a glass of water
to a thirsty person has to go,
we will see the people of this land living
in that mystical light again.
Turkmenistan, the refined land of the continent,
where there is a willingness of people
to come forward for
a prosperous tomorrow,
remembering the rustic but poor past,

3

Now, listen to the poor
and those who are willing to endure hardships
in search of a few truths.
You should look back
on the lives of those with eyes
that are staring at the high mountains
with open hearts and ears.
The age of persecution will pass.

**Waiting for the future time
when the boundaries collapse,
picking up those who have come back from
a distant trip, and be at the end of this road
and dancing together will surely come from here.**

Brunei

The people of Kampung Ayer,
the gardens on the old waters,
where they made a tent on the way
to the Pacific Ocean, gathered together
in a gorgeous gold crown
and talked about the future of the sea.
They laid down the fatigue of a long journey
in their smiles standing like this.
Where you've been in your dreams,
when discarding your selfishness
and your narrow minded heart,
and welcoming guests from far away countries,
the boundaries of this place will collapse
and peace will come. Have you met a good man?
It is a man who has no desire and is just looking,
but his heart is wide and humble.
Today I look at the blue sea
where the sun rises from
the floor of the house built on the water.

2

I put the traveler's tired journey here.
If any Gentiles can tolerate
and accept days for a forgiving mind,
the boundaries will collapse

and new times will wait for them,
and the people here will always live
with warm aura.
Hiding the hearts of hatred
and persecution under the shrinking waters,
touching the sick wounds of the good men
who came back from a long journey,
and remembering their names,
will come in this little land too.

Timor-Leste, East Timor

Do not forget the days of pain and suffering.
The brothers scattered on that day will gather
together to repair the fallen wall,
and will return to the house
without forgetting the sound of the flute of
the shepherd in childhood,
and the beautiful years will come soon to heal
the fallen roof and live together.
Let's not forget the wrinkled face of
the old mother who greeted the brothers
who left the house.
On the east side of the sea
where the sun always sets,
we will meet the sad music
and the dancers to comfort
the sad memories of the day.
Whistling, we will share our stories
and even the children of the opposite
side of the world.

2

The future must always be a man
who is now tearing his eyes
as if it is the gift of God coming suddenly to
those who are dreaming and preparing now,

and who has mercy on those
who are on that street today.
In the forest saw a small humming bird,
Small, but sincere birds that live
by collecting honey every petal.
Is not it beautiful?
It should not be forgotten.
Do not go through the day without meaning.
Plan and realize.
Do not just go through all the things
you meet in the woods,
you have to give your eyes
and have a meaningful time.

3

We should not forget the souls of those
who fell on the streets.
Do not forget those written
on the inscription without a name.
The wind must carry their stories
and tell us stories of the day
when we will cross the sea
and hear from us.
The poet should remember
and the land's rebirth will always be
the day of reunion with the dreamers
and the faces of those who miss the places
like the dew of morning.

Maldive Islands

When we go to the island,
our borders disappear
and we see a space
above the sea covered with fog.
It dreamed of a small empire,
a place where tribal peoples of
ancient pearls beneath the sea lived,
and the sky with its humid steam.
There was a firm willingness
to reestablish their collapsing boundaries
in a sudden whirlwind.
It sprinkled thousands stars.
After passing through the sea, we saw,
the islands people inhabited
by the atolls were not slaves.

2

The freedom of the island was not just given.
The people there seemed to enjoy peace in it.
We heard stories hidden in those old ages
that had found a lot of roads
on the sea rather than on land.
We walk the coast of Maldives today.
We walked through the traces
of glorious light down day and night,

**and everybody had a warm afternoon there,
feeling the heart that had come and went once.**

Iran

I followed the cold, snowy mountain range.
No mountain beast welcomed us.
The end of the wind was cold,
the tears were poured out,
and the night was hurried by hunger and cold,
and barefooted up the mountain.
Where are all those old people leaving?
Where are the friends
who were waiting here for us
and toasting together?
We had to listen to
the sound of falling down every night.
The cries of a crying child
and the slender breath of her mother
who could not comfort him.
The day of the dynasty
that was splendid was gone.
Memories were too much for us.
Oh, do you hear the cries
and whips of a horseman trying
to cross a frozen lake?
Did you see the traces of human pride
and selfishness buried
on the top of a high mountain?

2

The full moon was the night
that floated through
the gray buildings of Tehran.
In one of the old gardens,
there was a funeral ceremony
for the end of life.
Tomb of the Undocumented,
who never came to see
the flowers in their gardens.
In the blue light in the moon
and the face of a child who was lost his parent,
there was a colorful royal palace of the past.
In that form we heard their cries.
I can not go back.
And now I could not stand
in the air with my breath.
The stories I heard in the forgotten palace,
the still sound of the sitar
that revolves around my ears,
Going beyond the high mountains of Damavand.

3

If you think the road to go uphill is harsh,
you should look at the majesty of
the fallen comrades
and the majestic appearance of

the towering mountain peaks.
Look at the firm spirit that never breaks.
Today we are there, and in all the stillness,
when we open the closed door through
the cleansing ceremony
and greet the weary traveler on a long journey,
this garden will be as pleasant
and beautiful as an amusing wedding feast.

Artsakh Republic

Stepanakert,
look at the eagle holding that magnificent
and courageous sky holding our mountains.
They flew out of the serene country of the woods
and brought down the rain of abundance
on the high ground,
and people dreamed of the future.
The last days of pain will be engraved
on a brilliant pattern,
and a firm will -will be given to the little ones
under the mountain.
Look at the wheat field in that land.
Look at the fruit of the vineyard growing
in the hands of the farmer.
Do not forget this place wherever you go.
Artsakh,

2

In this black garden,
what else should we wait for?
The sunset can be seen from anywhere,
and the nostalgic people can not see it anywhere.
In the place where scattered and roots are drawn,
the daylight of the day stays for awhile,
disappears into the foothills of the mountains,

and the scars of war remain in this garden
where death and life repeat.
The wind blows in their garden,
where people leave and hope to harvest
their remaining spirits.

About the Author

Yongjea John Han majored in Law and English Literature, majoring in theology in the Netherlands and the United States. He also worked as a poet and writer in Korea and Canada.

(www.amazon.com/author/yongjeajohnhan)

www.ingramcontent.com/pod-product-compliance
Lightning Source LLC
Chambersburg PA
CBHW031151160426
43193CB00008B/329